First Concepts

Sticker
Words

How to use this sticker book...

Look at the pages

Find the stickers

Have lots of fun!

Toys

blocks

train

soldier

ball

dinosaur

digger

doll

aeroplane

rocking horse

Pets

fish

rabbit

tortoise

kitten

mouse

budgerigar

puppy

hamster

guinea pig

circle

heart

squares

diamond

triangle

oval

rectangle

star

Shapes

Clothes

hat

trousers

socks

sunglasses

dress

t-shirt

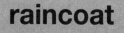

shoes

cardigan mittens raincoat

Home

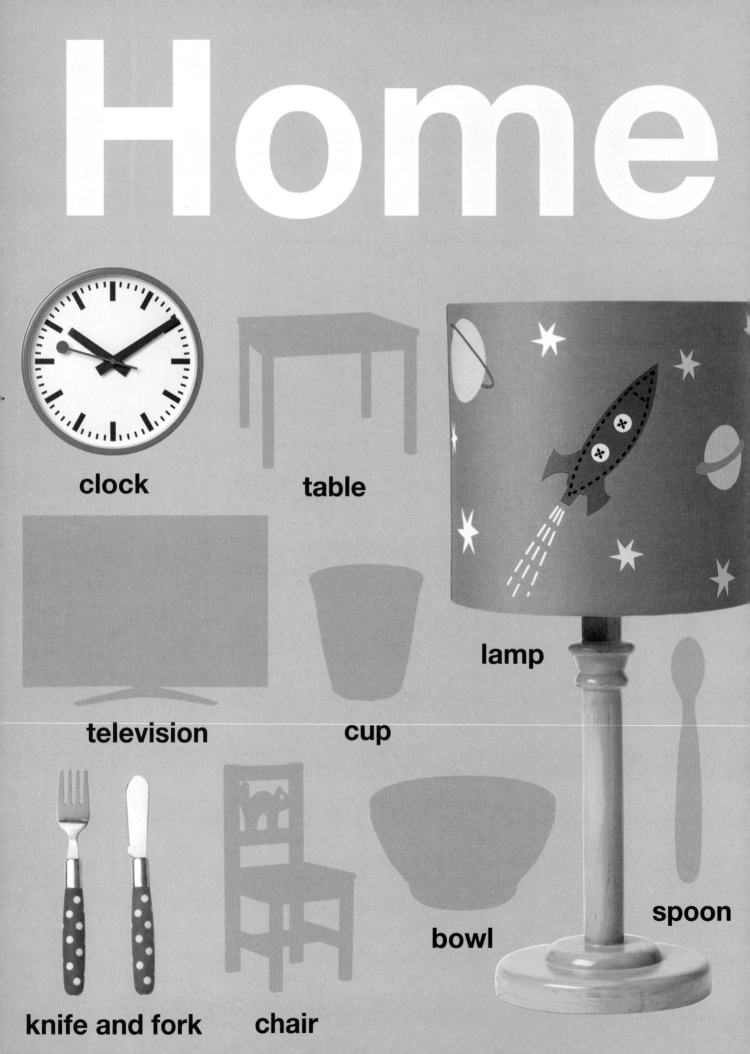

clock

table

lamp

television

cup

knife and fork

chair

bowl

spoon

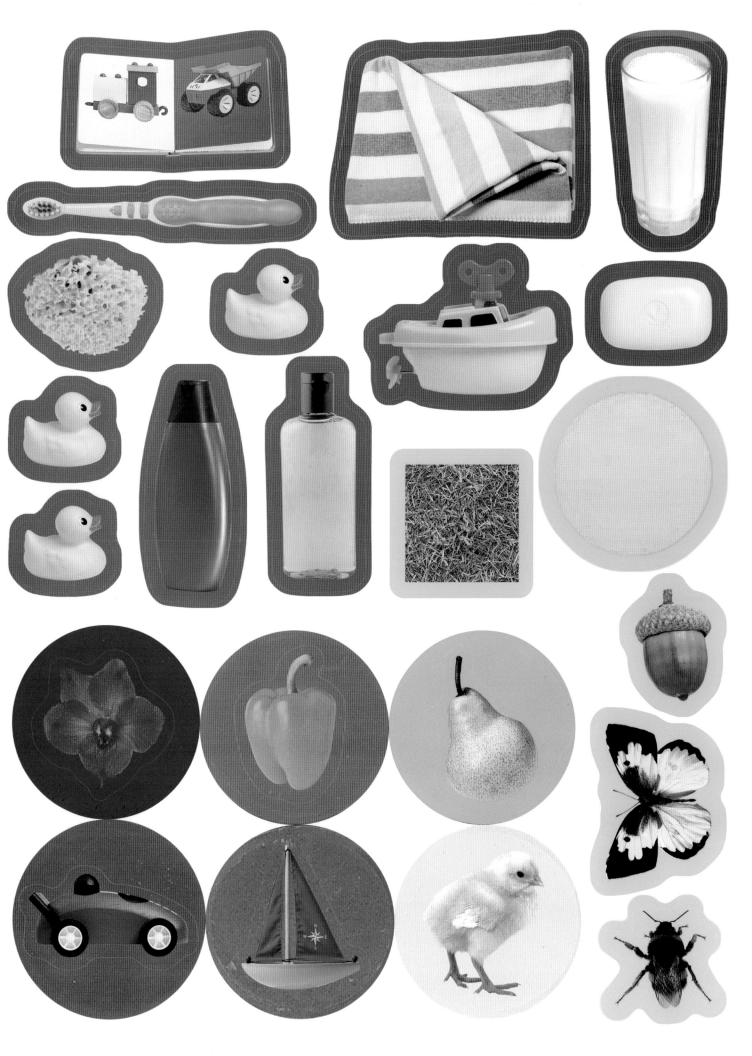

These stickers are for fun.

At my
House

Find the stickers to complete the scene.

cat

bird

flowers

window

dog

door

tricycle

Mealtime

eggs

chocolate

cheese

broccoli

apple

strawberry

juice

orange

banana

bread

book

bed

slippers

milk

pyjamas

toothbrush

blanket

teddy bear

pillow

Bedtime

Bathtime

sponge

shampoo   bubble bath

soap

tap

bathtub

boat

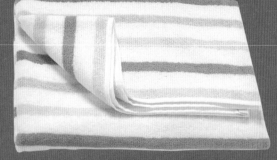

towel

ducks

Outside

sun

cloud

butterfly

slide

acorn

grass

bee

tree

sandpit

Colours

purple flower

orange pepper

green pear

yellow chick

blue boat

red car

Can you find the stickers that match the colours?